PETER JOHNSON

COVENTRY LIBRARIES

ROMANO-BRITISH MOSAICS

SHIRE ARCHAEOLOGY

Published by Shire Publications Ltd,
Midland House, West Way, Botley, Oxford OX2 0PH.
(www.shirebooks.co.uk)

First published 1982. Second edition 1987. Reprinted with amendments 1995
and 2002. Transferred to digital print on demand 2011.
Number 25 in the Shire Archaeology series.
ISBN-13: 978 0 85263 891 0.

*Cover: The Ganymede mosaic at Bignor Roman Villa, West Sussex. It shows the young
Trojan prince Ganymede being abducted by the god Jupiter to be his cupbearer on
Mount Olympus. Jupiter has disguised himself as a large eagle.
(Photograph courtesy of the Tupper Family, Bignor Roman Villa, West Sussex.)*

Coventry
City Council

CEN*

3 8002 01774 198 6		
Askews & Holts	Sep-2012	
738.520936 ADULT	£6.99	

It is a pleasure to ...... or their help in the
preparation of this ...... elp in updating this
edition, Mrs Patric ...... storical Monuments
(England) for help ...... avid Neal for advice
on copyright for h ...... osaics was warmly
fostered as a post ...... for his continuing
encouragement and ......
Finally, special tha ...... l suggestions about
the manuscript, to Luigi Thompson for the distribution maps and to Tracey Yeomans for
painstakingly transforming my scrawl into a typescript.

Printed in Great Britain by PrintOnDemand-Worldwide.com, Peterborough, UK.

Contents

Preface

This book is a basic introduction to the mosaics of Roman Britain. The text does not dwell in detail on the design development, art history or description of mosaics and readers eager to pursue these aspects are advised to consult the bibliography.

Later geometric mosaics are referred to relatively briefly. Although most recorded mosaics belong to this category, significant regional and historical developments cannot be adequately discussed in a volume of this size. Consequently figured mosaics, around which much of the work on fourth-century schools has been based, receive most attention.

Although 'school', a term of art historical origin, has become widely accepted, *officina*, i.e. 'workshop', is probably more appropriate and is used here throughout.

Preface to the second edition

There is a new chapter on mosaic recording, conservation and research to take into account recent advances, particularly in the organisation of conservation and research. The bibliography has been expanded and brought up to date and the list of sites to visit has also been revised. There are four extra plates mostly of new discoveries of mosaic.

For this new impression the bibliography has been revised and updated and a number of amendments have been made to the text.

List of illustrations

1
Introduction

Mosaic pavements are probably the most tangible and spectacular remains of the Roman occupation of Britain. The world 'mosaic' derives from *opus musivum*, the ancient term for wall-mosaic, associated originally with caves dedicated to the Muses. As early as the sixth century BC patterned pavements were being made in Greece from natural pebbles, but true mosaic paving, *lithostroton*, made from tailored coloured stones juxtaposed to produce patterns, did not appear until the third century BC in Greece and Sicily. Stone pavements primarily had a utilitarian function as a permanent floor covering and may have originally been inspired by carpet designs. Inevitably, however, this most durable of media was absorbed into the mainstream of Graeco-Roman art. Ultimately, in the imperial age, mosaic was literally elevated in prestige as decoration for the walls and vaults of bath-buildings and subsequently of early-Christian churches.

Within two decades of the Roman invasion of Britain in AD 43 mosaics were being laid by imported mosaicists. Over the next three centuries, however, there evolved a distinctive provincial and eventually insular tradition of polychrome mosaic. This, nevertheless, remained thoroughly classical in inspiration as the Celtic tradition never exerted the influence on mosaic that it did on other artistic media. Roman mosaics illustrate the classical obsession with order and symmetry and, because of the Roman abhorrence of a vaccum, maintained a rigid hierarchy of composition; consequently mosaic repertories remained relatively conservative.

Of over 1,500 mosaics, complete and fragmentary, recorded from Britain since the seventeenth century, most are now destroyed, 'lost' or otherwise inaccessible. Thus the tantalising fragments preserved in museums and, occasionally, *in situ* are a very small sample of the dazzling range of mosaics created in Roman Britain. Many, quite simply, were discovered too soon. The antiquarians of the seventeenth to nineteenth centuries took great delight in uncovering these pavements, often leaving a quaint description or fanciful drawing before allowing their discoveries to decay. A notable exception was Samuel Lysons, the eighteenth-century excavator and publisher of the Woodchester and Bignor villas and numerous other mosaics. His superb coloured engravings and meticulous descriptions of mosaic pavements in their architectural contexts were an inspiration to his

contemporaries.
Discoveries of Roman mosaics continued apace throughout redevelopment in the nineteenth century but these invariably were summarily treated as art objects or even curios. Only recently has iconographic study revealed mosaics to be not merely a series of attractive though obscure images but rather evidence for the degree of Romanisation of the province.

Since the early 1960s research has concentrated on the art history of Romano-British mosaics. This has been dominated by the work of Dr David Smith, who has demonstrated through the systematic analysis of designs and motifs that several 'schools' of mosaic flourished in Britain. More recently, emphasis has been given to design and construction methods and to the study of mosaics in relation to the buildings for which they were designed.

Plate 1.
Reconstructed
mosaicist's
workshop,
Corinium
Museum,
Cirencester.
(Photograph by
courtesy of
Judges Ltd,
Hastings.)

2
Design, construction and materials

The architectural historian Vitruvius described in the first century AD how to prepare the bedding for a mosaic floor. His elaborate formula, however, is rarely encountered when mosaic *substrata* are examined, for pavements were laid on foundations of widely differing quality. Quite commonly second-century mosaics were more soundly bedded than later examples. Usually, a pounded gravel base was prepared to receive concrete, *opus signinum* or lime mortar in layers of ascending fineness. The stones of the mosaic, the *tesserae,* were set into the final layer of mortar and grouted with a slurry of fine mortar.

There were three methods of mosaic construction, a combination of which could have been used for any one pavement.

Direct method

The *tesserae* were laid individually on to a fresh bed *in situ.* Usually the central part was laid first, then work would have proceeded outwards. This method was suitable for plain tessellated pavements and for simple motifs and repeating borders. Linear patterns such as guilloche could be quickly executed using registration *tesserae* at regular intervals. Alternatively, a template would have been used; one made of lead was discovered on the island of Delos. One small area at a time would have been laid and battens used to maintain straight edges for the precise abutment of subsequent work. Rulers, T-squares and pairs of compasses would have been the commonest tools used (plate 1).

Prefabrication: indirect method

The *tesserae* were laid on to a levelled bed of fine sand in a tray on which design lines had been etched. On completion, a sheet of linen (or paper) was glued to the upper surface of the tessellation and the panel was lifted from the tray and inverted between boards. The *tesserae,* now face down, were liberally coated with fine mortar and the panel was again inverted. The mosaic panel, now face up, was slid off the board into position on the damp mortar bed. After an interval the linen backing was peeled off as the animal glue was softened with hot water. The mosaic was then 'rubbed in' with a block of wood while water was occasionally sprinkled on the surface. The mosaicist

applied pressure to the block to force the mortar up between the
tesserae, which should have eventually stood proud of the mortar
when the surface was wiped down. A final grouting of fine mortar was
often added, pink being a popular colour. The indirect method enab-
led figured compositions and more elaborate motifs to be assembled
at relative leisure in the workshop.

Prefabrication: reverse method

A linen cartoon was used on which the design of the panel had been
drawn in mirror image. The *tesserae* were glued face downwards on
to the cartoon, coated with fine mortar and the whole inverted
between boards. The procedure was then the same as for the indirect
method. Reverse prefabrication had the advantage in that finer and
more intricate designs could be drawn on to a cartoon than could be
scratched into sand. Thus the finest work, apart from *emblemata*, was
best achieved using this method. The drying out and steady hardening
of a lime mortar bed would not facilitate the creation of fine works of
art *in situ*.

The *emblema*, the original prefabricated panel, was first developed
in the Hellenistic period when tiny *tesserae* were mortared directly
into a tray of marble or terracotta. This was then set into a tessellated
or mosaic floor as its centrepiece with the flange of the tray
deliberately visible, like a picture frame. A flourishing trade developed
with *emblemata* artists working on the grand scale. These artists tried
to imitate wall painting in composition and tone by using the technique of *opus vermiculatum,* so-called as the sinuous lines of fine
tesserae were worm-like. No true *emblemata* have been found in
British mosaics although the term is often loosely applied to most
prefabricated panels which should strictly be described as 'disguised
emblemata'. This disguised prefabrication is usually only detectable
when mistakes have been made. Occasionally one can see lines of
truncation in a border or pattern where a section has been cut to fit as
on the Brantingham pavement (plate 40), where a section of interlaced
circle pattern has been laid the wrong way round and awkwardly
abuts against another. Sometimes a circular panel was laid on the
wrong axis, as at Bignor and Brading, where masks of Medusa have
been set slightly off-centre, an easy error when working 'blind' with a
circular panel. The Hunting Dogs mosaic from Dyer Street,
Cirencester, probably incorporated two prefabricated masks of Neptune (plate 15). The unusual lack of symmetry in the spandrels
suggests that these masks were in short supply so the conventionalised flower and guilloche mat with *peltae* were inserted. Also, the
crenellated pattern below the sea-leopard was apparently cut to fit.

Marks made where panels abutted were observed in the bedding of a mosaic from Cirencester. Concentric circular guidelines were scratched into the beddings of the Rudston Charioteer and Hinton St Mary mosaics, probably to position prefabricated sections. Red pigment was observed following the outline *tesserae* of the marine creatures of the Littlecote mosaic, possibly the impression left by the cartoon, although, conversely, this could be from an outline for direct work. Although prefabrication would have been used for much figured work, crude work such as the Rudston Venus (plate 23) and the Bignor Medusa mosaics (plate 21) was obviously laid direct. Simple borders and the outer band of coarse tessellation would have been completed direct as would the bulk of the background *tesserae* in figured panels. Figures would have been prefabricated with at least two rows of background *tesserae* following the design contours.

A large mosaic pavement would entail several months' cartoon preparation and prefabrication in the workshop followed by several weeks' work on site. A permanent *officina* would only be needed if prefabrication was extensively practised. Once the new mosaic pavement was completed, the ceilings and walls would be plastered and painted and a quarter rounding or fillet of plaster would seal the junction between wall plaster and pavement. Only then would the mosaic be cleaned of limescale accumulated during the decoration of the room. This was achieved using a heavy stone with water as lubricant and sand as abrasive. One such rubbing block, of quartzite, has been found at Littlecote Park.

Today Roman mosaics are dampened to heighten the colours for photography and in the Roman period they were possibly waxed or oiled for the same effect, depending on personal taste. Repairs were necessary after a long period of wear; indeed Antonine mosaics at *Verulamium* were still in use at the beginning of the fourth century. Standards of repair are notoriously variable. The medallion of Autumn from Dyer Street, Cirencester, was crudely patched with *opus signinum* (plate 13) whereas an attempt was made to restore the design of the Colchester North Hill mosaic, albeit clumsily (plate 9).

Sometimes the work of different craftsmen is detectable on the same mosaic. The central panel of the Cupid mosaic at Fishbourne was well constructed yet the monochrome *canthari* of the spandrels were awkwardly drawn, probably by apprentices *(discipuli)* working direct (plate 18). It was probably the master who executed the polychrome work and left his bird 'trademark' in the scroll (plate 19).

Materials
Romano-British mosaics were constructed mostly from local

materials. The three 'primary colours' of mosaic, red, white and blue, dominated almost every scheme although the subtle juxtaposition of pastel shades added variety.

Some common colours and materials:

white, cream: hard chalk, oolithic limestone, carboniferous limestone.

reds, orange: chopped brick and tile or samian vessels, Old Red Sandstone, Purbeck marble.

blues: Lias limestone, shale, Purbeck marble.

black, greys: shale, reduced interiors of bricks and tiles.

pink: chalk, sometimes burnt.

purples, greys, browns, greens: Pennant sandstone.

greens: Lower Greensand, Purbeck marble.

browns: argillaceous limestone, ironstone.

Occasionally, imported marble was used, possibly from masons' offcuts. The Seasons mosaic from Cirencester (plate 13) and the Dionysus mosaic from Leadenhall Street, London (plate 17), contain marble *tesserae*. Glass tessarae, usually cut from green or blue bottles, were sometimes used as highlights, as in the birds' tails and gladiators' costumes at Bignor (plate 24). Loose gilt glass *tesserae* have also been discovered. Sizes of *tesserae* varied considerably. Generally, the larger the design, the larger the *tesserae*; thus those in the Great Pavement at Woodchester, about 750,000 of them, are on average 12.5 millimetres ($1/2$ inch) across. In contrast, the *tesserae* of the Bignor gladiators are only 4 to 5 millimetres ($3/16$ inch) across.

Slabs of stone were cut up in the in the workshop by saws with smooth iron blades, using sand and water. More manageable sheets of material were brought to the site and *tesserae* manufactured in temporary workshops.

Knapping areas have been identified at Rudston, *Durobrivae* and at Littlecote, where piles of unused *tesserae* and their chippings were found sorted into colours. Softer material such as chalk was sawn into sticks, as found at Corfe Castle, Dorset, and in the *forum* at Silchester. To obtain *tesserae*, the sticks were held on the edge of a chisel embedded in a block, against which a hammer was struck (plate 1). Similar tools were found at Silchester. The pincers favoured by modern mosaicists may also have been used, although there is no evidence for this.

Design

The increasing sophistication of geometric designs and figured schemes argues strongly for professional mosaic designers. The *musivarius* supervising the laying of the mosaic may often have been executing schemes adapted by a designer from a pattern book. These were apparently produced for various artistic media and each mosaic *officina* would have produced its own repertory book literally with guidelines to aid its mosaicists. Neal suggests that there would been a different book with suggested completed schemes for the client to choose from. Slavish copying from cartoons or repertory books was seldom practised as only rarely are two mosaics found exactly like. The adapted design had to take account of room dimensions and client's specifications in iconography, although most designs were apparently chosen at random. Only occasionally was a mosaic designed specifically for a room, as at Littlecote, Keynsham, Frampton and Hinton St Mary.

Geometric designs were, in the main, elaborations of simple repeating schemes such as grids and interlaced polygons. These and compass-drawn schemes such as the Colchester Middleborough mosaic needed guidelines to be etched into the damp bedding irrespective of construction method. With the Colchester mosaic, Crummy has demonstrated how the compass lines would also have aided construction of the superposed triangle pattern in the spandrels, here probably direct (plate 8).

Pattern-book designs had to be scaled up to fit a particular room. The Middleborough mosaic was designed in multiples of 2 1/2 Roman feet as an aid to such calculations.

Several inscriptions in mosaics indicated that mosaic was paid for by the foot although cost must have been dictated by the degree of complexity and quality of the work. Cato, writing in the second century BC, tells us that the client would provide or pay for the materials and pay the craftsman only for his labour, but obviously some flexibility in this was exercised. Diocletian's Price Edict of AD 301 indicates that painters were paid rather more than mosaic workers: the wall painter (*pictor parietarius*) was prescribed a daily wage of 75 *denarii*, half as much again as the floor mosaicist (*tessellarius*). Even the more prestigious *musearius* (wall and vault mosaicist) received only 60 *denarii*. All this suggests that mosaic was considered the inferior medium and that the *tessellarius* was not normally the designer – in fact, with rare exceptions (plate 25), he remained anonymous.

Plate 2. Exeter, c AD 60. Polychrome mosaic from legionary baths. (Photograph by courtesy of Exeter Archaeological Field Unit.)

Plate 3. Fishbourne, West Sussex. Lozenge design in Italian black and white tradition, AD 75-80. (Photograph by courtesy of Judges Ltd, Hastings.)

3
First-century beginnings

The earliest dated mosaic from Britain is that from the bath-house of the legionary fortress at **Exeter** *(Isca Dumnoniorum)*, built *c* AD 55-60. The largest surviving fragment apparently shows the forelegs of a horse galloping towards the sun (plate 2) while another fragment has the remains of a *cantharus*. A representational polychrome mosaic of this date is remarkable as is the use of samian *tesserae*. The work, though colourful and lively, lacks the expertise of later mosaic. Smith has suggested a military mosaicist; if so, he was probably an artisan attached or contracted to the Second Legion *Augusta*. Another probable first-century mosaic was laid in the fortress bath-house at **Caerleon** *(Isca Silurum)*.

The bulk of the first-century material is formed by the unique series of mosaics from the Flavian palace at **Fishbourne**, West Sussex, dated to AD 75-80. Some sixty to seventy mosaics were laid in this lavish Italianate structure and eighteen of them survive at least in part. The Fishbourne series is so distinctive that it should be considered as an isolated phenomenon, in a class by itself. These mosaics exerted little discernible influence on the British tradition, apart from the later floors at Fishbourne itself, and are clearly the work of mosaicists trained in Gaul or Italy.

The repeating patterns of the monochrome floors, based mainly on interlaced polygons forming lozenges, have close parallels in late first-century mosaics from Gaul, notably Besançon. The designs are formal, yet some variety is provided by the elaborate filling motifs, though the standard is less accomplished than that of later British mosaics. One particularly attractive mosaic from a private suite of the palace remained in use into the third century (plate 3). The design, based on boxes, crosses and lozenges, gives the effect of false perspective. Restrained filling motifs of superposed triangles, conventionalised flowers and solids do not reduce the overall impact of the design. One of these austere Flavian pavements was discovered in 1980 beneath the Cupid on a Dolphin mosaic, which had been lifted for conservation. Although badly robbed and collapsed in antiquity the design was restorable (plate 4). This had a grid of sixteen panels, each containing a different repeating arrangement of simple motifs including wedges, triangles and tilted boxes. The borders of the mosaic provide the main interest, however. A continuous ashlar pattern sur-

SECOND PERIOD MOSAIC IN ROOM 7

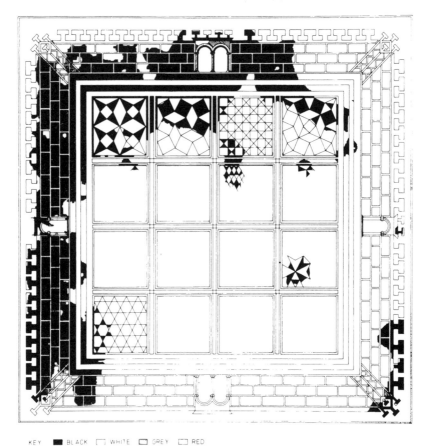

KEY   ■ BLACK   ☐ WHITE   ☐ GREY   ☐ RED

Plate 4. Fishbourne. Fortress mosaic, AD 75-80. (Reconstruction drawing by David Rudkin, by courtesy of Sussex Archaeological Society.)

mounted by T-shaped crenellations is pierced on each side by a gateway, while each corner has a turret. Clearly these are the stylised defences of a town or fortress. Designs of this type apparently originated in the first century AD and became popular throughout the empire.

The sober black and white floors of the palace would have contrasted sharply with the brilliantly coloured wall plaster. A small number of the Flavian mosaics were polychrome however, including a concentric circular design with solidly coloured strands of guilloche. Fishbourne as a palace was exceptional and only three villas in Britain have produced evidence for first-century mosaic: **Rivenhall** in Essex, **Angmering** in West Sussex and **Eccles** in Kent. The *frigidarium* of the Eccles bath-house was paved with a polychrome mosaic, surviving as fragments, tentatively reconstructed by Neal as a pair of gladiators in combat within a square of three-strand guilloche, surrounded by a perspective box design. The baths are dated to AD 65-120 but the elaborate polychrome guilloche and figured work suggest a date nearer to 120 than 65, perhaps before 100.

The first evidence for urban mosaics is from **London** *(Londinium)*. Before the end of the first century a house excavated in Watling Court had been decorated with polychrome mosaics, one of which had a marine scene. It is hardly surprising that cosmopolitan London provided the demand and attracted the expertise for mosaics in this early period.

Plate 5. *Verulamium,* St Albans. Shell mosaic, *c* AD 130-50. (Courtesy of Verulamium Museum.)

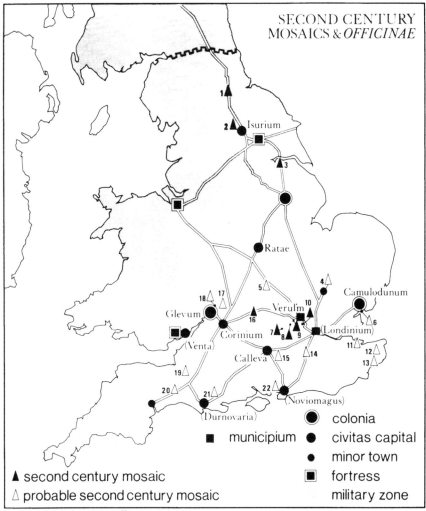

SECOND CENTURY
MOSAICS & *OFFICINAE*

- ⬤ colonia
- ◼ municipium
- ⬤ civitas capital
- ● minor town
- ▲ second century mosaic
- ◼ fortress
- △ probable second century mosaic
- military zone

Fig. 1. Second-century *officinae* and mosaics. Named towns are bases for *officinae*. Names in brackets are probable bases for *officinae*.
Key. 1 Piercebridge villa, Durham. 2 Well-in-Bedale, North Yorkshire (Isurian *officina*). 3 Winterton, South Humberside (Isurian *officina*). 4 Great Chesterford, Essex, temple. 5 Mileoak villa, Northamptonshire: first to early second century. 6 West Mersea, Essex (probably *Camulodunum officina*). 7 High Wycombe, Buckinghamshire *(Verulamium officina)*. 8 Latimer, Buckinghamshire, Room 27 *(Verulamium officina)*. 9 Boxmoor, Hertfordshire *(Verulamium officina)*. 10 Park Street, Hertfordshire *(Verulamium officina)*. 11 Faversham, Kent. 12 Wingham, Kent: late first to early second century. 13 Folkestone, Kent. 14 Walton Heath, Surrey. 15 Crondall, Hampshire. 16 North Leigh, Oxfordshire, Room 30 *(Verulamium officina)*. 17 Wadfield Farm, Gloucestershire. 18 Great Witcombe, Gloucestershire, Room 5. 19 Littleton Villa 2, Somerset. 20 Combe St Nicholas (Wadeford), Somerset. 21 Dewlish, Dorset, Room 25 (beneath aquatic mosaic). 22 Fishbourne, West Sussex, probably Cupid mosaic. *Venta* = Caerwent.

4
Second-century expansion

The stimulation of town life following Hadrian's visit in AD 121 or 122 promoted a demand from the new curial class for polychrome mosaics for their comfortable town houses. This demand was met by new urban *officinae,* operating at their peak from AD 150 to 190, whose predominantly geometric repertories assumed a distinctly British character. As early as *c* AD 130-50 the apsidal room of a house in *Verulamium* (**St Albans,** Hertfordshire) received an expertly constructed mosaic (plate 5). The design imitated a fluted scallop shell bordered by wavecrest pattern and was provided with a broad expanse of red-brick tessellation.

The Antonine period was the heyday of the *Verulamium* mosaicists, one of whose most accomplished works graced a courtyard house. This curvilinear adaptation of a compass-drawn scheme has as its focal point a panel with a lion carrying off the bloodied head of a stag (plate 6). The musculature is skilfully rendered, yet the heads of the animals show a confusion of detail. Typically British is the lack of formal background apart from a stylised shadow. The lion's tail is truncated, suggesting prefabrication. The spandrels contain elegant *canthari* with distinctive swastika shading and the design is skilfully linked by tightly designed chain guilloche. The outer coarse tessellation, broad even by British standards, was for the location of furniture and also reduced the cost.

This hybrid design is closely paralleled by the mosaic from Middleborough, **Colchester** *(Camulodunum),* also dated to the late second century (plate 7). The central panel has the remains of two wrestling Cupids watched by a bird. The spandrels are filled by rather mundane vegetable motifs, staggered triangles and *peltae.* Chain guilloche is used but less tightly constructed than on the *Verulamium* pavement. The 'inhabited scroll' border contains several mistakes in the disposition of the motifs, which were intended to have an ordered repetition (plate 8). Crummy suggests these birds, ivy leaves and lotus flowers were laid by mosaicists not involved with the actual design, working direct; however, the central panel at least was probably prefabricated.

Smith has postulated a joint *Verulamium-Camulodunum officina.* It is perhaps more likely that each town was the base for an *officina* exchanging mosaicists or cartoons with the other. Certainly

Plate 6. *Verulamium.* Lion and Stag mosaic, late second century. (Copyright David Neal.)

Camulodunum has revealed a large number of mosaics (forty-six) for a town of only 108 acres (44 ha). Another probable result of *Verulamium-Camulodunum* liaison was a mosaic from North Hill, Colchester, dated to the middle of the second century (plate 9). This has a scheme of nine panels superimposed on one of concentric circles. The central roundel with the remains of a *cantharus* is framed by cornice pattern while each corner apparently contained a 'squared rosette', both being second-century innovations.

The adjoining panel, a scheme based on staggered octagons, was butted on to the main design probably only after a short interval. One surviving *cantharus* has swastika shading reminiscent of a vessel on the Lion and Stag mosaic. The main design, however, is repeated not only on another mosaic from the same *Camulodunum* house but also on a mosaic from *Verulamium* dated to AD 180-200. The last two have the same central motif of a many-petalled flower, the so-called '*Verulamium* dahlia', further evidence of co-operation between *officinae*.

Plate 7. Colchester, Middleborough. Wrestling Cupids, late second century. (Courtesy of Colchester Archaeological Trust.)

Plate 8. Colchester, Middleborough. Scheme by Philip Crummy showing the design in multiples of $2\frac{1}{2}$ Roman feet. (Courtesy of Colchester Archaeological Trust.)

Plate 9. Colchester, North Hill. Nine-panel design superimposed on a concentric circular scheme. Mid second century. (Copyright David Neal.)

Plate 10. Silchester. Hexagonal panel design produced by the Callevan *officina*. Second century. (Courtesy of the Society of Antiquaries of London.)
Plate 11. Silchester. All-over *maeander* design, Callevan *officina*. Second century. (Courtesy of the Society of Antiquaries of London.)

The *officina* operating at **Silchester** *(Calleva)*, Hampshire, during the second century had a more restrained, exclusively geometric repertory. A courtyard house in *Insula* XIV, dated to AD 140-60, is a typical Callevan residence, whose main wing received four well bedded and crisply executed pavements. One has a unique scheme of elongated hexagons whose interspaces contain tilted swastikas (plate 10). The contents of the hexagons have diagonal symmetry and include squared rosettes, cornice pattern and miniature scroll.

One mosaic from this house is in monochrome (plate 11). This all-over *maeander* design incorporates staggered squares with straight-forward geometric motifs. Like other Callevan pavements the threshold is marked by a simple geometric panel, here composed of tilted squares.

Leicester *(Ratae)* has also produced evidence for a second-century *officina*. The Blackfriars mosaic (plate 12) has an octagonal panel design containing samian *tesserae* cut from bowls dated to AD 125-

Plate 12. Leicester. Blackfriars mosaic. Dated by samian *tesserae* to *c* AD 150. (Photograph courtesy of Leicestershire Museums Service.)

Plate 13. Cirencester, Dyer Street Seasons mosaic. Dionysus as Autumn. Probably late second century. (Photograph by courtesy of Judges Ltd, Hastings.)

40; thus the pavement was probably laid soon after 150. The panels are filled with bifurcated-scale and staggered triangle patterns, all constructed with compass lines. The miniature scroll and cornice pattern accord with a second-century dating.

A second octagonal panel design from *Ratae*, the St Nicholas Street mosaic, is strikingly similar in design and workmanship. This is dated by samian *tesserae* to c AD 155 and is clearly a product of the mosaicists responsible for the Blackfriars mosaic. This *Ratae officina* must have been responsible for the fragmentary geometric mosaics from the Blue Boar Lane town house of Antonine date.

Octagonal panel designs originated in the second century and remained popular into the fourth. Another probable second-century example is the Seasons mosaic from Dyer Street, **Cirencester** *(Corinium)*, Gloucestershire. This, unusually, has wholly figured panels with mythological characters, suggesting a slightly later date. This Dionysiac mosaic features elegant male representations of the Seasons, of which Autumn (plate 13) ranks amongst the finest mosaic

Plate 14. Cirencester, Dyer Street. Marine *thiasos*. Probably late second century. (From Lysons, 1817)

'portraits' from Britain. His windswept hair is garlanded with fruits partly made from glass *tessarae*. The Hunting Dogs mosaics also from the Dyer Street house was evidently prefabricated, as discussed above (plate 15). The central panel was apparently repaired in antiquity. The tessellated patch obviously replaced a damaged figure who was pursued by the pack of dogs, one of which was also destroyed. Their quarry was probably Actaeon, punished for seeing Diana at her toilet.

A third mosaic from this *Corinium* town house and *officina* was a marine tableau which Toynbee rightly considers to be the most classical of Romano-British mosaics (plate 14). Lyson's engraving shows a sea-leopard, a *hippocampus* and other marine fauna all elegantly designed. The remains of a nereid riding on the tail of a sea monster and a Cupid holding the wheel of what must have been Neptune's chariot are elements of what was probably a marine *thiasos*.

As already seen, houses in **London** received mosaics from an early period. The Leadenhall Street pavement, one of the finest recovered from the city, may be second-century although an early third- or fourth-century date cannot be ruled out (plate 17). The fine central panel of Dionysus reclining on a tiger is bordered by twisted ribbon,

wavecrest and an unusual shaded saw-tooth pattern which is reproduced exactly on a mosaic from Bucklersbury, another product of the *Londinium officina.*
The second-century mosaic boom also reached the north. A mosaic from **Aldborough** *(Isurium),* North Yorkshire, which has as a centrepiece an eight-petalled flower, is assignable to the second century (plate 16). This and another mosaic from the same town house, featuring a lion basking beneath a tree, were doubtless from the same workshop. The stepped *maeander* of the illustrated example is paralleled on a corridor mosaic from **Winterton,** South Humberside, dated to *c* AD 180, another likely product of this putative Isurian *officina.* This may also have been responsible for geometric mosaics, including one with cornice pattern, from nearby **Well** villa, said to date to the second century.

At **Fishbourne,** the first-century Fortress mosaic was overlaid by another with a central panel featuring a Cupid riding a dolphin (plate 18). This has been dated by samian *tesserae* to AD 150-200, although

Plate 15. Cirencester, Dyer Street. Hunting Dogs mosaic. Probably late second century. (Photograph by courtesy of Judges Ltd, Hastings.)

Plate 16. Aldborough, North Yorkshire, 1848. Late second-century mosaic from an Isurian town house. (From Smith, H. E., 1852, *Reliquiae Isurianae.*)

an early third-century date is a possibility. Two opposing lunettes contain sea-panthers in polychromy whereas the others contain *hippocampi* in the by then decadent Italian black and white tradition.

Relatively few villas have produced firm evidence for second-century mosaic. At **Latimer,** Buckinghamshire, a fragment was dated to AD 150-60 and at **High Wycombe,** in the same county, a nine-panel design featuring the Seasons was dated by samian *tesserae* to AD 150-75. These and the second-century mosaics from **Boxmoor**

Plate 17. London, Leadenhall Street, Dionysus reclining on a tiger. Probably late second or early third century. (From Roach Smith, C., 1859, *Illustrations of Roman London.*)

and **Park Street** in Hertfordshire, all close to *Verulamium*, have led Smith to suggest that the *officina* there extended its operations into the countryside during the Antonine period (fig. 1).

Plate 18. Fishbourne, West Sussex. Cupid on a Dolphin mosaic. Late second or early third century. (Photograph by courtesy of Judges Ltd, Hastings.)
Plate 19. Fishbourne, West Sussex. Cupid mosaic. Scroll with mosaicist's trademark. (Photograph by Raymond Thomas, courtesy of Sussex Archaeological Society.)

5
Third-century depression

After AD 200 the craft in Britain declined abruptly and seems to have lapsed completely between AD 230 and 270. This slump is not unique to Britain as most of the western empire suffered a recession in mosaic production during this period.

Despite the dearth of British mosaics firmly dated to the third century the hiatus is not so complete as was once thought. Two villa excavations have produced external evidence for third-century mosaics although little survived of these pavements. Work at **Latimer,** Buckinghamshire, revealed a simple mosaic, black diamonds on a white ground, dated not earlier than c AD 210-20, and another, surviving only as loose *tesserae,* dated AD 232 to c 250. Additionally, a fragmentary mosaic from **Rapsley,** Surrey, is dated to AD 220-80 (plate 20). The restored design, based on lozenges and forming L-pieces, occurs throughout the empire from the second to the fourth centuries and here indicates some continuity of tradition. A small number of mosaics has been assigned a less specific third-century date on external evidence such as the fragmentary apsidal mosaics from Wollaston House, **Dorchester,** and **Kenchester** *(Magnis)* in Herefordshire.

Doubt has been cast over the dating of the later pavements at Fishbourne, including the Cupid on a Dolphin mosaic, which admittedly is inconclusive. Smith suggests that many of these are more likely to be third-century than second.

Comparison with continental material is restricted by the insular character of British mosaics. Polarisation in dating has led to many mosaics being automatically assigned to the second or fourth century. Occasionally, however, the opposite occurs when a mosaic exhibiting no obvious trait of either period is placed in the third century, for example the curious Medusa and Seasons mosaic from **Bignor** (plate 21). This is obviously not part of the superb late series from the villa and, more significantly, is partly overlaid by steps leading up into the later villa extensions. This, together with pottery found when the mosaic was relaid in 1974, strongly indicates a third-century date.

The Venus mosaic from **Rudston,** North Humberside, has been assigned to the fourth century, yet subsequent external evidence indicates that it was laid before AD 300 (plate 23). The design, normally described as compass-drawn, was here obviously drawn freehand though with a wide range of colours. This wild-looking Venus, accom-

Plate 20. Rapsley, Surrey. Mosaic dated A D 220-80. (David Neal and Crown Copyright.)

panied by a merman (?) holding a torch, has dropped her mirror to grasp at her golden apple. The lunettes contain animals apparently from the arena, two accompanied by Latin inscriptions, 'the spear-bearing lion' and 'the man-eating bull'. The spandrels feature nude *bestiarii,* hunters from the arena, and each long side-panel has a grotesque representation of Mercury (?) flanked by vines. Despite appallingly clumsy draughtsmanship the figures possess an undeniable vitality and represent sophisticated though as yet obscure iconography. Smith has suggested that the animals are Seasonal; in-

Plate 21. Bignor, West Sussex. Medusa and the Seasons, third century. (From Lysons, 1817.)

Plate 22. Aldborough, North Yorkshire. Wolf and Twins mosaic, possibly third century. (Photograph by the author, with acknowledgement to Leeds City Museum.)

deed the overall theme of the mosaic appears Dionysiac.

A crude mosaic from **Aldborough** may also be of third-century date (plate 22). This shows a charming she-wolf, about to suckle Romulus and Remus beneath a tree, a job for which she is supremely ill equipped.

These stylised mosaics were probably the work of jobbing artisans after the urban *officinae* had gone out of business. Often described as naive, these pavements nevertheless vividly demonstrate the thoroughness with which classical culture had permeated the fringes of the empire.

The second-century *officinae* must have so saturated the market that demand fell with the end of the building boom. The earlier mosaics were attractive and so well constructed that obsolescence would have been retarded. The inflation and anarchy of the third century were no doubt factors in the slump for while towns were being fortified there would have been little cash for luxuries. It was not until the closing years of the century that Britain began to emerge from the depression.

Plate 23. Rudston, North Humberside. Venus with hunters and beasts of the arena. Before *c* AD 300. (Photograph by courtesy of City of Kingston upon Hull Museums.)

6
Fourth-century revival

Towards the end of the third century many Romano-British villas began to assume a new architectural sophistication. It has been argued elsewhere that this was caused by a 'flight of capital' from the continent as a result of barbarian incursions into eastern Gaul from AD 260-75. The new landowning aristocracy elaborated existing villas and established new ones. The ensuing demand for fine mosaic pavements must have been met initially by continental craftsmen who subsequently helped establish new *officinae*.

This astonishing British revival of mosaic art is most evident in the south and south-west where the concentration of villas is most dense. Recovery also took place in the towns, however, as for example the series of mosaics laid *c* AD 300 in *Verulamium*. Whereas second-century mosaics were predominantly geometric the reverse was the case in the fourth century, when figured work came to the fore.

By *c* AD 300, or shortly after, some villas were refurbished with sophisticated polychrome mosaics, for example **Bignor,** West Sussex, which has the finest series of mosaics known from Britain. The apsidal chamber has a mosaic with a medallion of a nimbed goddess flanked by elegant gamebirds and *cornucopiae,* below which is an exquisite frieze of Cupid gladiators practising under the eye of their trainer (plate 24). The goddess has variously been identified as Venus and Juno but more reasonably is Diana, patron deity of the amphitheatre. The figured Bignor mosaics are the work of the master mosaicist who left his 'signature' in one of the floors (plate 25). His name might have been Terentius and he must have learned his skills in Gaul.

According to Johnston, the Bignor floors belong to the **Central Southern Group,** whose products are concentrated in Berkshire, Hampshire and Sussex. No focus for this series is identifiable yet, though Winchester *(Venta Belgarum)* and Chichester *(Noviomagus)* are strong candidates. Alternatively these mosaics were produced by separate teams of mosaicists who influenced one another. The closest extant parallels for Bignor are the geometric mosaics from **Sparsholt,** Hampshire, and **Chilgrove,** West Sussex, the latter dated to the early fourth century, which must be the later work of Terentius or his pupils.

Smith has postulated four fourth-century schools of mosaic, the most vigorous in the north-western provinces being that based at

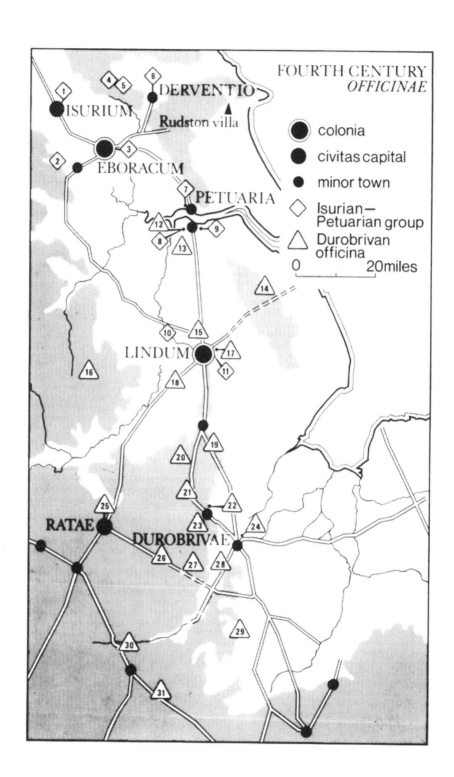

FOURTH CENTURY
OFFICINAE

● colonia

● civitas capital

• minor town

◇ Isurian—
  Petuarian group

△ Durobrivan
  officina

0 _____ 20miles

ISURIUM

DERVENTIO

Rudston villa

EBORACUM

PETUARIA

LINDUM

RATAE

DUROBRIVAE

Plate 24. Bignor, West Sussex. Apsidal panel with Diana and Cupid gladiators. Probably c AD 300. (From Lysons, 1817.)

Cirencester *(Corinium)* in Gloucestershire. This comprised two *officinae,* the first of which devised a distinctive Orpheus mosaic with a concentric circular design. Britain has the greatest concentration of Orpheus mosaics in the empire, perhaps as many as fourteen, at least four of which are Corinian products. One of the earliest is from the

Fig. 2 *(left).* Fourth-century products of *officinae* in the north.
Isurian-Petuarian Group. 1 Aldborough *(Isurium).* 2 Dalton Parlours, West Yorkshire. 3 York *(Eboracum),* Micklegate Bar. 4 Beadlam, North Yorkshire. 5 Hovingham, North Yorkshire. 6 Malton *(Derventio),* Seasons mosaic. 7 Brantingham, North Humberside. 8 Winterton, South Humberside, several including Orpheus mosaic. 9 Horkstow, South Humberside. 10 Sturton, Lincolnshire. 11 Lincoln *(Lindum).*
Durobrivan officina. 12 Winterton, South Humberside, fragments found 1958. 13 Roxby, South Humberside. 14 Kirmond-le-Mire, Lincolnshire. 15 Scampton, Lincolnshire. 16 Mansfield Woodhouse, Nottinghamshire. 17 Greetwell Fields, Lincolnshire. 18 Norton Disney, Lincolnshire. 19 Haceby, Lincolnshire. 20 Denton, Lincolnshire. 21 Thistleton Dyer, Leicestershire. 22 Great Casterton, Leicestershire. 23 Tixover Grange, Leicestershire. 24 Castor (Mill Hill), Cambridgeshire. 25 Leicester *(Ratae),* several. 26 Medbourne, Leicestershire. 27 Great Weldon, Northamptonshire. 28 Cotterstock, Northamptonshire. 29 Great Staughton, Cambridgeshire. 30 Nether Heyford, Northamptonshire. 31 Bancroft, Buckinghamshire.

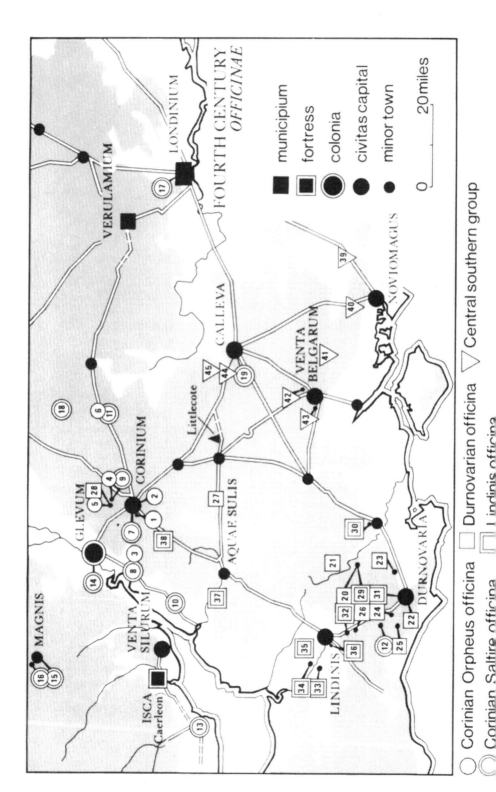

MAGNIS

VERULAMIUM

LONDINIUM

17

18

6
11

CORINIUM

GLEVUM

5 28
4
9
2
1
7
38
3
8
14

VENTA
SILVRUM

10

ISCA
Caerleon

13

37

LINDINIS

34
33

35

36

32
20
26
29
24
31

21

23

22

12
25

30

DURNOVARIA

AQUAE SULIS

27

Littlecote

45
44
19

CALLEVA

42

43

VENTA
BELGARUM

41

40

39

NOVIOMAGUS

16
15

FOURTH CENTURY
OFFICINAE

municipium

fortress

colonia

civitas capital

minor town

0   20miles

Corinian Orpheus officina   Durnovarian officina   Central southern group

Corinian Saltire officina   Lindinis officina

villa at **Barton Farm** just outside Corinium, dated to shortly after AD 300 (plate 26). Here Orpheus is seated on a rock with his lyre, accompanied by a small fox-like dog, commonly featured with him in Romano-British mosaics. He is encircled by a register of birds, a distinctive wreath of laurel and an outer register of wild beasts. These powerfully drawn animals, mostly big cats, pad along in subdued fashion, possibly lulled by Orpheus' music but more in the manner of a Dionysiac procession.

The master of the Barton Farm mosaic was obviously responsible for the magnum of the *officina*, the Great Pavement at Woodchester, Gloucestershire (plate 27). This mosaic, at almost 15 metres (50 feet) square the largest north of the Alps, paved the audience chamber of a palatial villa. It shares with Barton Farm mosaic the laurel wreath and the registers of subdued birds and beasts, in procession and alternating with stylised trees. Elaborations include the outer *acanthus* scroll proceeding from a mask of Neptune and the spandrels containing pairs of nereids with water plants, against a blue background. The marine theme was continued at the centre of the mosaic which, according to antiquarian references, featured fish swimming about a star. These may have been surrounded or been at the bottom of a marble pool or fountain, as only something structural could have displaced Orpheus from the customary central position. The area outside the column bases comprises twenty-four geometric

Fig. 3 *(left)*. Products of fourth-century *officinae* in the south.
Corinian Orpheus officina. 1 Barton Farm, Gloucestershire. 2 Cirencester *(Corinium)*, Dyer Street. 3 Woodchester, Gloucestershire. 4 Chedworth, Gloucestershire. 5 Withington, Gloucestershire. 6 Stonesfield, Oxfordshire.
Corinian saltire officina. 7 Cirencester *(Corinium)*, several. 8 Frocester Court, Gloucestershire. 9 Chedworth, Gloucestershire. 10 Tockington Park, Avon. 11 North Leigh, Oxfordshire. 12 Halstock, Dorset. 13 Llantwit Major, South Glamorgan. 14 Gloucester *(Glevum)*, Bon Marché (Northgate Street), 1914. 15 Kenchester *(Magnis)*, Herefordshire. 16 Bishopstone, Herefordshire. 17 London *(Londinium)*, Old Broad Street. 18 Wigginton, Oxfordshire. 19 Silchester *(Calleva)*, *Insula* XXVII, Building 1, Room 27.
Durnovarian officina. 20 Fifehead Neville, Dorset, 1903. 21 Hinton St Mary, Dorset. 22 Dorchester *(Durnovaria)*, several. 23 Dewlish, Dorset. 24 Wynford Eagle, Dorset. 25 Frampton, Dorset. 26 East Coker, Somerset. 27 Cherhill, Wiltshire. 28 Withington, Gloucestershire.
Lindinis officina. 29 Fifehead Neville, Dorset, 1880. 30 Hemsworth, Dorset. 31 Dorchester *(Durnovaria)*, Colliton Park. 32 Lufton, Somerset. 33 Low Ham, Somerset. 34 Pitney, Somerset. 35 Littleton, Somerset, Villa 1. 36 Ilchester Mead, Somerset. 37 Keynsham, Avon. 38 Kingscote, Gloucestershire.
Central Southern Group. 39 Bignor, West Sussex. 40 Chilgrove, West Sussex. 41 Bramdean, Hampshire. 42 Itchen Abbas, Hampshire. 43 Sparsholt, Hampshire. 44 Silchester *(Calleva)*, *Insula* XXVII, Building 1, Room 18. 45 Basildon, Berkshire.

Plate 25. Bignor, West Sussex. Dolphin panel and signature of the master mosaicist, probably Terentius, who may have trained in Gaul. (Photograph by the author, with acknowledgement to J. Tupper.)

Plate 26. Barton Farm, Cirencester. Mosaic of the Corinian Orpheus *officina*. After *c* AD 300. (Photograph by courtesy of the Warburg Institute.)

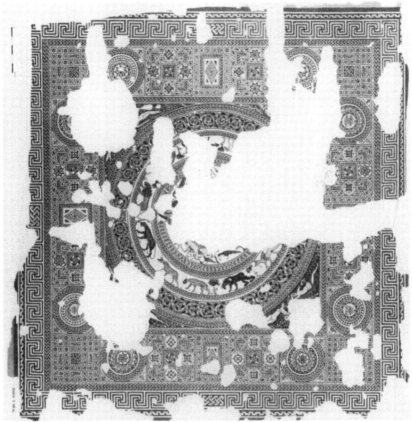

Plate 27. Woodchester, Gloucestershire. The Great Pavement, Corinian Orpheus *officina*. Early fourth century. (David Neal and Crown Copyright.)

panels featuring lozenge patterns, concentric circular schemes or *maeander* patterns.

The Orpheus *officina* produced the fine *triclinium* mosaic at **Chedworth,** Gloucestershire (plate 30). This features the Corinian *acanthus* scroll issuing from elegant *canthari*. These panels flank an all-over *maeander* design with inset guilloche mats, another Corinian device. This geometric area would have accommodated dining furniture and was no doubt separated from the figured area by an archway. Originally, eight trapezoid panels forming an octagon contained pairs of mythological lovers alternating with dancing *bacchants* and *maenads* in Dionysiac revelry. Each corner panel contained a Cupid in the guise of a Season.

Plate 28. The Wotton Mosaic, stone for stone replica and restoration of the Great Pavement at Woodchester. (Photograph by courtesy of Bob Woodward.)

A later Corinian Orpheus mosaic from **Withington,** Gloucestershire, is noticeably different to the others in arrangement and style (plate 29). Other mosaics from the villa, however, clearly derive from the Corinian repertory, thus the mosaicist of the Withington Orpheus was probably inspired by the work of his predecessors.

The second and partly contemporary Corinian *officina* specialised in saltire schemes and their derivatives. **Halstock** villa in Dorset is an outlier in Durotrigan territory (plate 31). This repeating saltire design has the characteristic *peltae* with convoluted terminals, budded knots and basin-shaped *canthari*. The 'saltire-derivative' schemes at **Kenchester** *(Magnis)* and **Bishopstone** in Herefordshire, **Llantwit Major** in South Wales and Old Broad Street in **London** were presumably the work of itinerant mosaicists contracted to the saltire *officina*.

The fragmentary mosaic from **Frocester Court,** Gloucestershire, dated after *c* AD 340, on stylistic grounds is one of the latest products of the *officina*, thus the two Corinian *officinae* probably operated over the first half of the fourth century.

The school whose postulated centre was **Dorchester** *(Durnovaria)*, Dorset, specialised in sophisticated pavements with mythological scenes and marine compositions. These pavements, mainly in Dorset and Somerset, were probably the work of two *officinae* operating with some overlap and liaison in the *civitas* of the Durotriges. Indeed, Smith has already suggested an offshoot of the 'Durnovarian school' based at **Ilchester** *(Lindinis)*, which became the second Durotrigan capital in the third century. Here we will refer to the former grouping or school as the **Durotrigan Group** with *officinae* at *Durnovaria* and *Lindinis*. The Durnovarian *officina* produced the well known

Plate 29. Withington, Gloucestershire. Corinian Orpheus mosaic of the first half of the fourth century with later insertion of the Neptune panel by the Durnovarian *officina*, probably *c* AD 350. (From Lysons, 1817.)

Plate 30. Chedworth, Gloucestershire. *Triclinium* mosaic with Dionysiac scenes. Corinian Orpheus *officina*. (Photograph: Royal Commission on Historical Monuments (England).)

Christian mosaic from **Hinton St Mary,** Dorset (plate 32). The central medallion contains a striking portrait of a clean-shaven young man with soulful eyes, superimposed against a Christogram: the only known representation of Christ in a mosaic pavement. The multiple borders suggest a late date; indeed Reece has demonstrated that the decadent hairstyle of Christ has parallels on coinage dated to *c* AD 335-55. The lunettes contain hounds chasing deer against a stylised background of trees and Toynbee interprets these as scenes of paradise. The quadrants feature busts of young men identified as the Evangelists. Curiously, the right arm and shoulder of each has been compressed as if by afterthought *(in situ?)*. The languid eyes of men and beasts, the leafy scrollwork and skilfully interconnected guilloche are Durnovarian hallmarks.

Painter has demonstrated that the design probably originated as a painted ceiling decoration, thus Christ *Pantocrator* would have gazed down from a domed ceiling.

The Hinton St Mary mosaic and the lost mosaics from **Frampton,** also in Dorset, are obviously by the same master mosaicist. An apsidal panel at Frampton contains a Christogram set within a scroll

Plate 31. Halstock, Dorset. Mosaic of the Corinian saltire *officina*, first half of the fourth century. (Photograph: Ted Flatters, by courtesy of Ron Lucas.)
Plate 32. Hinton St Mary, Dorset. Christ and the Evangelists, Durnovarian *officina*. Probably *c* AD 335-55. (Photograph by courtesy of the Trustees of the British Museum.)

opposite what should be described as a chalice rather than a *cantharus* (plate 33). The damaged central roundel featured, as in an adjacent mosaic at Hinton, Bellerophon slaying the Chimaera, i.e. a triumph of good over evil. The lunettes, vandalised in antiquity, apparently featured marine scenes and the corner panels, also partly destroyed, contained pairs of mythological lovers. A tessellated Latin epigram, flanking a mask of Neptune from which issues a procession of dolphins, refers to the realm of Neptune, i.e. the marine scenes. A second epigram flanking a Cupid refers to the realm of 'mightier Cupido', i.e. the pairs of lovers. The master mosaicist or designer and his client evidently had no qualms about juxtaposing Christian symbolism and a blatantly pagan repertory.

Plate 33. Frampton, Dorset. Christian mosaic with scenes of classical mythology. Durnovarian *officina,* mid fourth century. (From Lysons, 1813.)

Plate 34. Hemsworth, Dorset. Venus rising from the sea. *Lindinis officina,* fourth century. (Photograph: Royal Commission on Historical Monuments (England).)

A late example of Durnovarian work was laid at **Withington** (plate 29). One side flanking the Corinian Orpheus mosaic was removed to accommodate a series of marine panels when the chamber was extended around the middle of the century. Evidently, as the Corinian *officinae* were no longer in business, mosaicists were commissioned from *Durnovaria,* expanding northwards but whose work had deteriorated slightly.

A Durnovarian mosaic from **Dewlish** dated after AD 353 proves that this *officina* survived into the second half of the fourth century. The *Lindinis officina* was responsible for the mosaics at **Hemsworth,** Dorset, one of which featured the birth of Venus from the sea (plate 34). This has a procession of dolphins of a type virtually identical to those on a mosaic from **Fifehead Neville** attributed to Durnovarian mosaicists. This or the Hemsworth mosaics, however, must be the first products of mosaicists once based at *Durnovaria* and newly transferred to *Lindinis.* Marine subjects, a Durnovarian forte, were to feature prominently in the Lindinian repertory. Not surprisingly, mythological scenes became another speciality of the *officina*, such as at **Keynsham**, Avon. The conjectural *apodyterium* of the hitherto unlocated bath-house had the only figured mosaic at the villa. One of its very fine panels shows Europa

Plate 35. Kingscote, Gloucestershire. Venus mosaic. Probably *Lindinis officina*, fourth century. (Photograph: Royal Commission on Historical Monuments (England).)

Plate 36. Keynsham, Avon. Europa and the Bull, fourth century. (Photograph by courtesy of Cadbury Limited.)

garlanding a bull, Zeus in transformation (plate 36). This mosaic features an unusual chevron pattern also paralleled at Hemsworth.

Other products of the *Lindinis officina* include the fine figured pavements at **Pitney, Low Ham** and **Lufton,** all within a few miles of *Lindinis*. Lindinian mosaics from Low Ham and **Colliton Park,** Dorchester, both dated to after AD 340, indicate that this *officina* was broadly contemporary with that based at *Durnovaria*.

The mosaic from the settlement at **Kingscote,** Gloucestershire, may result from the northern expansion of the *officina* into former Corinian territory (plate 35). As at Hemsworth Venus is featured but

Plate 37. Roxby, South Humberside. Lozenge design of the Durobrivan *officina*, third quarter of the fourth century. (Engraving by Fowler, number 3.)

here in a portrait medallion of such skill that prefabrication must have been used. The marine panel of the threshold, apparently asymmetric, features dolphins with convoluted tails and the remains of a sea monster whose neck is twisted backwards.

Whereas mosaics of the south, particularly in the second century, show more affinities with Gaul than with other provinces, those of the west country apparently owe more to Mediterranean and African influence. For example, the Corinian laurel wreath and *acanthus* scroll are more African as is the style, content and disposition of the panels in the mosaic from Low Ham. The frequent occurrence of Neptune, Venus and marine scenes in the south-west further suggests influence

Plate 38. Scampton, Lincolnshire. Corridor mosaic of the Durobrivan *officina*, third quarter of the fourth century. (Engraving by Fowler, number 8.)

from Africa, where they abound.

Whereas in this late period figured mosaics were exclusive to the west country, the south and the north, the mosaics of the East Midlands and most of Lincolnshire were, with rare exception, entirely geometric. Many of these were produced by the *officina* based at **Water Newton** *(Durobrivae)*, Cambridgeshire. Durobrivan mosaics were commissioned for over twenty sites from Lincolnshire to Buckinghamshire and several firmly dated mosaics indicate that this *officina* was trading during the third quarter of the fourth century. Tightly designed schemes based on eight-lozenge stars, grids, interlaced octagons and interlaced circles dominated the rather sober Durobrivan repertory.

A mosaic from **Roxby,** South Humberside, is representative, having an all-over lozenge-star scheme incorporating mats of guilloche and a central tilted square with conventionalised flower (plate 37). Outer borders of swastika-*peltae* and Z-pattern provide some variety. A comparable scheme occurs on the elaborate corridor mosaic from **Scampton,** Lincolnshire (plate 38). This incorporates swastika-*peltae* as filling motifs in an eight-lozenge star pattern. The outer border of large interlaced circles is paralleled on several Durobrivan mosaics. Mosaic distribution suggests that temporary workshops were set up in Lincoln *(Lindum)* and Leicester *(Ratae)* although headquarters remained at *Durobrivae*.

The northernmost school proposed by Smith, apparently based at

Brough-on-Humber *(Petuaria),* specialised in radial designs as at **Brantingham, Winterton** and **Horkstow,** all within a few miles of *Petuaria.* Subsequent attributions to this grouping, however, indicate that it covered a much wider area of Yorkshire and Humberside. As several of these attributable mosaics are from **Aldborough** *(Isurium)* and none at all from *Petuaria,* the series would be referred to more appropriately as the **Isurian-Petuarian Group,** although this description would have to be modified in the light of future discoveries. The *coloniae* of **York** *(Eboracum)* and **Lincoln** *(Lindum)* might be better candidates for *officinae* but only one attributable mosaic has been found in each. Alternatively, these mosaics were produced by itinerant craftsmen working from temporary bases.

Prominent in this group are the Orpheus mosaics of **Horkstow** and **Winterton,** only five miles apart. The Horkstow pavement is particularly impressive, having two radial schemes, one of which featured Orpheus with his dog surrounded by curvilinear registers of birds and beasts (plate 39). The central radial scheme, bordered by an obviously late eight-strand guilloche, is supported by four Titans. The panels contain as yet obscure figured scenes of ungainly draughtsmanship. Coloured backgrounds are used extensively, giving the impression of a painted ceiling.

At **Brantingham,** across the Humber, a radial scheme was adapted for an octagonal format, the 'spokes' of guilloche radiating from a figured medallion (plate 40). This featured a nimbed Tyche, patron deity of a town, set against a red background. Two rows of nimbed nymphs set into 'niches' of guilloche also have red backgrounds. In the eight lunettes *nereids* holding fronds recline against water jugs as at Woodchester. These, together with coloured backgrounds and the subject of Orpheus, strongly suggest influence from *Corinium,* although the languid eyes of Tyche resemble those of Christ from Hinton St Mary. Dated geometric pavements from Brantingham and Winterton indicate that the mosaicists of the Isurian-Petuarian Group probably operated towards the middle of the fourth century, when the Corinian *officinae* were beginning to decline.

Several geometric mosaics from **Aldborough** *(Isurium)* show affinities with those at Brantingham and Winterton. A corridor pavement discovered in 1770 (plate 41) has lozenges, as at these two sites, and an interesting 'striped chequer' paralleled at Brantingham and on a mosaic from **Sturton,** Lincolnshire (plate 42).

A mosaic from **Rudston** which would be out of place in this northern group may be a slightly later work (plate 43). The mosaic in the adjoining chamber apparently had a radial design but it is the surviving mosaic which is anomalous. This features a frontal represen-

Plate 39. Horkstow, South Humberside. Orpheus mosaic of the Isurian-Petuarian Group, mid fourth century. (Engraving by Fowler, number 2.)

Plate 40. Brantingham, North Humberside. Tyche mosaic of the Isurian-Petuarian Group, mid fourth century. (David Neal and Crown Copyright.)

Plate 41. Aldborough, North Yorkshire, 1770. Corridor mosaic with lozenges. Isurian-Petuarian Group, fourth century. (From H. E. Smith, 1852.)

Plate 42. Sturton, Lincolnshire. Isurian-Petuarian Group, fourth century. (Engraving by Fowler, number 11.)

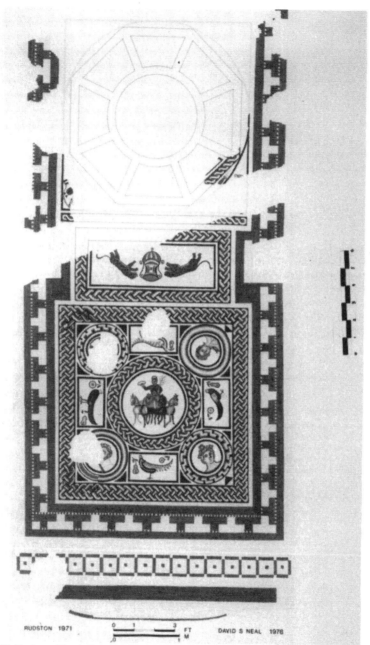

RUDSTON 1971   0 1   3 FT   DAVID S NEAL 1976
                0   1 M

Plate 43. Rudston, North Humberside. Victorious charioteer and the Seasons. The mosaicist was evidently familiar with the *Lindinis* repertory. Fourth century. (David Neal and Crown Copyright.)

Plate 44. Lenthay Green, Sherborne, Dorset. Apollo in musical contest with the ill fated Marsyas. Fourth century. (Photograph: Royal Commission on Historical Monuments (England).)

tation of a charioteer with his team, holding a wreath and palm as symbols of his victory. Seasons occupy the corner medallions, of which Spring (top right) is exceptionally fine and obviously the work of a master. Two opposing medallions are bordered by 'rainbow' pattern, also found around portrait medallions in Lindinian mosaics from Colliton Park and Lufton. It is feasible that the Rudston master was an itinerant mosaicist attached to the *Lindinis officina*.

Moreover, further stylistic considerations indicate an exchange of influence and artisans between the two regions during the second and third quarters of the fourth century. The mosaic from **Lenthay Green** near Sherborne, Dorset, has a representation of Apollo in a musical contest with the ill-fated Marsyas (plate 44). This crudely stylised work is reminiscent of mosaics from Aldborough and Rudston already discussed. The interlaced squares of guilloche and the use of chequer, however, suggest a fourth-century date for this pavement, which is more crisply executed than its northern counterparts.

Another late pavement of uncertain attribution is the Orpheus mosaic at **Littlecote Park**, Wiltshire, first discovered in 1727 and recently re-excavated and restored (see cover). This mosaic, however, in an unheated chamber set apart from residential structures, was more than mere decoration. Because of its iconography and architectural context this has been identified as the pavement of a private *temenos* devoted to the Orphic cult, a mystery religion that flourished during the brief pagan revival of the fourth century.

The mosaic, dated to *c* AD 360, typically had cryptic iconography and intentionally so. Walters, however, has demonstrated that Orpheus here acts as a link between Apollo, of whom he was priest, and Dionysus, the principal deity of the cult alluded to in the mosaic. The feline face in each apse is a solar image radiating beams of light and which, as the Orphic writings relate, became Dionysus by night. The goddesses reclining in front of running animals, zoomorphic transformations of Dionysus, are Seasonal, each playing a part in the Orphic mysteries.

Smith has suggested that the Littlecote mosaic belongs to a 'late Durno-Corinian phase of the Corinian school'. Certainly, it shows affinities with mosaics of the west country (and the north) such as several of the *Lindinis officina* and those from **Newton St Loe**, Avon, of disputable Corinian origin. This pavement was evidently laid at a time when the Constantinian *officina* system was breaking down. Some *officinae* enjoyed a brief expansion at the expense of others going out of business. We have seen that in this late period mosaicists were moving from region to region in search of new commissions. Mosaics, like the Littlecote Orpheus, of problematic attribution but of high standard, presumably reflect such activity.

After *c* AD 380 the mosaic craft began its final decline although mosaics of good quality were being laid at *Verulamium* and Gloucester *(Glevum)* in the last two decades of the century. The simple geometric pavements from **Hucclecote** in Gloucestershire, dated to after *c* 395, must be among the last produced in Britain.

7
Recording, conservation and research

The present standard of mosaic recording reflects the sophistication of modern archaeological techniques and easily surpasses that of previous eras. Since the late 1950s David Neal of the Historic Buildings and Monuments Commission has been producing paintings at 1:10 scale of mosaics discovered on state-sponsored excavations and on other Roman sites in Britain. These, together with new works, are now to form the basis of a Corpus of Romano-British Mosaics. This corpus will also be based on current work by Stephen Cosh who has also become a leading recorder and researcher of Romano-British mosaics.

More recently other artists and illustrators attached to museums and archaeological units have been using this and other techniques to achieve similar results. Luigi Thompson produces paintings, also at 1:10 scale, mostly of mosaics excavated in Wiltshire. His largest work has been the stone for stone recording of the **Littlecote** Orpheus mosaic (plate 46) showing the state of survival of the figured areas of the west chamber when excavated in 1978. He also recorded the fragmented geometric pavement discovered in the churchyard at Manningford Bruce near Pewsey, Wiltshire (plate 47). Exhaustive efforts to reconstruct it on paper have made clear that the scheme of interconnecting ovals and loops of guilloche is unique in Britain although paralleled in *Gallia Belgica* and other provinces in the second to third centuries. The **Manningford Bruce** mosaic was in such poor condition that it was reburied *in situ* for its protection.

Such accurately measured recordings are often invaluable guides in the conservation of mosaics, for example when reassembling lifted sections and for enabling accurate cartoons to be drawn up for the restoration of lost areas. Drawings, from which the final painting is produced, can be made in the field. Alternatively a photo-mosaic is made on site from overlapping vertical photographs taken over a string grid of, say, 20 cm intervals. Accurate paintings can also be produced from photographs of lost or reburied mosaics, even from oblique views. The final painting is invariably executed in restored colours, that is, the colours when the mosaic is dampened, using poster colours or artist's gouache. Final colour matching can be achieved in the studio using samples of dislocated *tesserae*. Stained *tesserae* are often restored to true colours and encrustations are normally omitted. The mosaic painting should provide more information than any photograph.

Plate 45. Cherhill, Wiltshire. Central panel of a large mosaic featuring a hunting dog bounding past a leafy tree. A late product of Durnovarian mosaicists expanding northwards around the middle of the fourth century. (Photograph: Roman Research Trust).

Conservation

Many mosaics were destroyed or damaged in the Roman period during rebuilding or demolition of the structure they decorated. In medieval times much destruction of mosaics took place, particularly at risk being those laid over hypocausts which were systematically robbed of tiles and stone. Pavements laid in unheated rooms, such as corridors, cult chambers and *frigidaria*, often escaped such vandalism, for example the mosaics at **Littlecote** and at **Low Ham** in Somerset. The mosaic re-excavated at **Cherhill** in Wiltshire in 1984, although from a large unheated chamber, was largely destroyed in post-medieval or modern times by construction of the forecourt of Cherhill Manor. The best surviving part (plate 45), featuring an obviously Durnovarian hunting dog running past a tree, as at **Hinton St Mary**, was lifted for conservation and is now displayed in Devizes Museum.

Mosaics are sometimes found subsiding into earlier features such as ditches and pits, some being so distorted as to be plunging vertically. It is nevertheless possible to record such mosaics and restore them to shape for museum display. There are two principal methods of lifting, usually dictated by the firmness of the underbedding and other factors. In both methods the mosaic is first secured by sticking gauze to its surface with water-soluble adhesive. The more common method is to lift

Plate 46. Littlecote Villa, Wiltshire. Part of the painting by Luigi Thompson showing Orpheus and the Seasons. (Copyright: Roman Research Trust.)

the mosaic in sections. Vertical cuts are made along the design lines to minimise ugly joints when the sections are reassembled. As the bedding is carefully undercut boards are slid underneath and the section lifted. The **Littlecote** and **Hinton St Mary** mosaics were lifted in this manner by Art Pavements and Decorations Ltd (then part of Carter Contracting), the leading specialists in this field.

The more spectacular method of lifting is rolling, possible only if the bedding is not too hard and the surface of the mosaic is level. The mosaic is rolled up, usually in one piece, around a reinforced drum while being slowly undercut. This was how the staff of Hull Museums lifted the **Brantingham** Tyche mosaic (plate 40) and the **Rudston** Charioteer mosaic (plate 43) for display in Hull Museum of Transport and Archaeology.

Mosaics that have been lifted for display in museums are nowadays rebacked with new strong but lightweight materials. Fibre-glass vermiculite and epoxy resin are used rather than the thick concrete favoured by the Victorians as a backing medium. Imaginative restoration of missing figured work is minimal in Britain although the outlines of damaged panels and other geometric areas are sometimes indicated by lines painted on the filling medium or by other means.

The ethics of mosaic conservation and restoration are often hotly debated. In some instances it is a question of taste as not everyone will agree on a particular manner of presentation. Individual sites and mosaics pose individual problems which should be assessed accordingly.

The **Fishbourne** mosaics were relaid by Art Pavements in the 1960s to their contours as excavated, that is, having subsided into the post holes and other features of earlier building phases. This is perhaps of more immediate benefit to archaeologists than to the lay public who can be confused by the undulating and plunging surfaces. However, due to 'stretching' of the tessellation, it would have been virtually impossible to relay the mosaic *in situ* as flat as first laid.

More controversial was the ambitious and unprecedented restoration of the **Littlecote** mosaic from 1979 to 1980, also by Art Pavements (see cover). This was only possible because of extremely fine recordings made when the floor was first uncovered virtually intact in the eighteenth century. Thus when the mosaic was re-excavated in 1978 it was possible to restore the missing areas very accurately. It was also practicable to display the mosaic *in situ* in its architectural context to demonstrate how such a mosaic would have appeared as first laid in the fourth century. A mosaic presented *in situ* in this manner is a permanent reminder that these pavements were intended to decorate standing Roman buildings and not just to grace the walls of modern museums. The sophisticated iconography of the Littlecote mosaic was clearly intended as a visual narrative for followers of the Orphic and Dionysiac cults. The reconstruction painting of the interior of the exotic double chamber (plate 48) shows how the Orpheus mosaic formed an integral part of the overall design. In this context many mosaics are to be seen as social documents, echoing the religious and philosphical currents of the late Roman world.

Too many other mosaics have been less fortunate and have deteriorated badly since discovery or are considered to be 'lost' or destroyed, as at **Frampton** (plate 33). Mosaics are very fragile and much has still to be done to create an awareness of undiscovered mosaics and the possible dangers to them. To this end the Association for the Study and Preservation of Roman Mosaics was created in 1978. ASPROM endeavours to monitor the condition of all Roman mosaics in Britain and to liaise with excavators, museums, archaeological societies, landowners and developers to recover and protect these art treasures. ASPROM is now the largest and most active national section of

Plate 47. Manningford Bruce, Wiltshire. Badly damaged geometric mosaic excavated in the churchyard in 1985.

Plate 48. Littlecote Villa, Wiltshire. Reconstruction painting of the interior of the Orphic hall, *c* AD 360. (Copyright: Roman Research Trust.)

L'Association International pour l'Étude de la Mosaique Antique (AIEMA), based in Paris and concerned with the art historical study of ancient mosaics. A parallel organisation is the International Committee for the Conservation of Mosaics founded in Rome in 1977, which promotes research research and training in mosaic conservation.

Current research

Mosaic research has concentrated in recent years on stylistic groupings and problems of dating. However, not all mosaics can be attributed to a theoretical school or *officina*; indeed only a small minority of mosaics surviving to any reasonable extent can be so classified. Recent research indicates a more complex situation than was considered in the 1960s, particularly in the alter Roman period. The more stylistic analysis that takes place the more blurred the picture becomes and, in all probability, the more close to reality.

Work by AIEMA, based at the Centre National de la Recherche Scientifique in Paris, has concentrated on a systematic survey of designs, patterns and motifs used throughout the Roman empire. This has resulted in a magnificent volume produced at CNRS with detailed illustrations of each design accompanied by a description of it in several languages (see Bibliography). Another major achievement of AIEMA and the CNRS is the creation of a computer databank on mosaic design elements. It is hoped that eventually information will be fed into the international databank, from where it could be tapped by any authorised resaercher with access to a compatible computer terminal.

For many years national corpora of the mosaics of Gaul, Spain, Tunisia and other provinces have been produced in regional volumes. It is gratifying to be able to report that the publication of a four-volume corpus of mosaics of Roman Britain, by Drs. David Neal and Stephen Cosh, has recently been completed under the auspices of ASPROM. Research on mosaic iconography and mosaics as related to room function has continued to gather pace in recent years, led in particular by members of ASPROM such as Roger Ling, Patricia Witts and Anthony Beeson. More work though needs to be carried out on geological analysis of mosaic tesserae which has considerable potential for the economics of the craft.

8
Major collections of Roman mosaics

Visitors are advised to find out opening times well in advance of travel.

Aldborough, North Yorkshire (YO51 9EP). Second-century geometric mosaics preserved *in situ* close to the museum. Telephone: 01423 322768.
Website: www.english-heritage.org.uk

Bath, Somerset. Roman Baths Museum displays the Weymouth House School geometric mosaic and *Blue Coat School* aquatic mosiac. Telephone: 01225 477785.
Website: www.romanbaths.co.uk.

Bignor, West Sussex (SU 9814). Large courtyard villa with superb figured mosaics, laid around AD300. Telephone: 01983 869259. Website: www.bignorromanvilla.co.uk

Brading, Isle of Wight (Po36 0EN). Villa with sophisticated figured mosaics, probably fourth-century. Telephone: 01983 406223. Website: www.bradingromanvilla.org.uk

The British Museum, London. Prominent is the central roundel of the mosaic from *Hinton St Mary*, featuring a depiction of Christ. Also the Dionysus mosaics from *Leadenhall Street* and *Thruxton*, Hampshire, and the Durnovarian panel from *Withington*. Telephone: 020 7323 8299. Website: www.thebritishmuseum.org

Chedworth, Gloucestershire (GL54 3LJ). Villa with fine Seasons mosaic and a Corinian saltire mosaic. Telephone: 01242 890256. Website: www.nationaltrust.org.uk

Cirencester, Gloucestershire. Corinium Museum has the *Hunting Dogs* and *Seasons* mosaics and the fourth-century *Hare* mosaic. Also the *Barton Farm* Orpheus, the *Kingscote* Venus and a reconstructed mosaicist's workshop.
Telephone: 01285 655611. Website: www.cotswold.gov.uk

Colchester, Essex. Colchester Castle Museum displays the second-century *North Hill* mosaic and a fourth-century radial mosaic from *Lion Walk*. Telephone: 01206 282939.
Website: www.colchestermuseums.org.uk

Devizes, Wiltshire. Wiltshire Heritage Museum displays the hunting dog panel from the *Cherhill* mosaic. Telephone: 01380 727369. Website: www.devizes.org.uk

Dorchester, Dorset. Dorset County Museum has the fourth-century geometric mosaics from *Durngate Street, Olga Road* and the *Gaol*, possibly from the third-century, Neptune mosaic from *Fordington High Street* and a fourth-century aquatic panel from *Dewlish*. The fourth-century *Colliton Park* town house is displayed *in situ*, with geometric mosaic, behind the County Hall. Telephone: 01305 262735.
Website: www.dorsetcountymuseum.org

Fishbourne, West Sussex (SU 8404). The earliest series of mosaics in Britain decorates this Flavian palace. Later floors include the Cupid on a Dolphin mosaic.
Telephone: 01243 789829. Website: www.sussexpast.co.uk

Hull, East Yorkshire. Hull and East Riding Museumhas the fourth century mosaics from *Rudston, Brantingham* and *Horkstow*.
Telephone: 01482 300300. Website: www.hullcc.gov.uk

Leicester, Jewry Wall Museum displays the second-century *Blackfriars* and *St Nicholas Street* mosaics, the *Cyparissus* panel and the fourth-century *Norfolk Street* 'shell' mosaic. Telephone: 0116 252 8915. Website: www.leicester.gov.uk/museums

Littlecote Park, part of Littlecote House Hotel, near Hungerford, Berkshire (RG17 0SU). The hotel is owned and managed by Warner Hotels. The spectacular mosaic of the villa's orphic *temenos* has been extensively restored *in situ*. Telephone: 01488 682509. Website: www.warnerukhotels.co.uk

Lullingstone, Kent (DA4 0JA). Villa with fourth-century mosaics featuring Bellerophon and the Chimaera and Europa and the Bull. Telephone: 01322 863467. Website: www.english-heritage.org.uk

Museum of London. The Bucklersbury mosaic now paves a reconstructed *triclinium*. Telephone: 020 7001 9844. Website: www.museumoflondon.org.uk

North Leigh Villa, Oxfordshire (OX29 6QE). A Corinian saltire mosaic is displayed in a *triclinium*. Telephone: 0870 333 1181. Website: www.english-heritage.org.uk

Reading, Berkshire. Museum and Art Gallery has many mosaics, mostly second-century, from *Silchester*. Telephone: 0118 937 3400. Website: www.readingmuseum.org.uk

St Albans, Hertfordshire. Verulamium Museum displays the second century *Lion and Stag, Oceanus* and *Shell* mosaics. An Antonine mosaic and a panel of *c*.AD 300 are displayed *in situ* in Verulamium Park. Telephone: 01727 819340. Website: www.stalbansmuseum.org.uk

Taunton, Somerset. The Museum of Somerset has the fourth-century Virgilian mosaic from *Low Ham* and the Hunters mosaic from *East Coker*. Telephone: 01823 278805. Website: www.somerset.gov.uk/museums

Winchester, Hampshire. City Museum displays mosaics from *Middle Brook Street* and *Little Minster Street* and fourth-centurygeometric mosaic from *Sparsholt*, Hampshire. Telephone: 01962 848303. Website: www.winchester.gov.uk/heritage

York, Yorkshire Museum displays Seasons mosaic from *Toft Green* and the Medusa mosaic from *Dalton Parlours*, West Yorkshire. The Hospitium in the Museum Gardens contains a curious mosaic from *Oulston*, North Yorkshire. Telephone: 01904 650333. Website: www.yorkshiremuseum.org.uk

In addition to sites and venues for mosaics, students of mosaic should note the *David J Smith Archive*. This reference collection of books, corpora, mounted photographs and ephemera on ancient mosaics throughout the world can be visited in a dedicated room in the Joint Library of the Hellenic and Roman Societies. This archive was a gift by Dr David Smith to the Roman Research Trust. It is kept up to date by purchases of specialist material funded by the Roman Research Trust and is a unique resource for scholarship.

Telephone: 020 7862 8709.

Website: www.icls.sas.ac.uk/library/About/Collection

9
Glossary

Acanthus: prickly plant conventionalised in scroll form (see *Scroll*).

Antonine: reign of emperor Antoninus Pius, AD 138-61, here including the reigns of Marcus Aurelius, AD 161-80, and Commodus, AD 180-92.

Apodyterium: changing room of a bath-house.

Apse: semicircular (i.e. apsidal) extension to a room.

Bacchant(e): wine-loving celebrant of the mysteries of Dionysus. See *Maenad.*

Basilica: classical public building with central nave and aisles, some later converted into churches.

Cantharus: wine cup with handles, a Dionysiac symbol much used in Roman art.

Cartoon: design of mosaic panel outlined on cloth or paper, for use in prefabrication.

Christogram: monogram of Christ, formed from the first two letters (chi-rho) of the Greek *Christos.*

Civitas capital: centre of a tribal area or *civitas.*

Colonia: city originally settled by legionary veterans (except *Eboracum*).

Constantinian: strictly, the reign of Constantine I, AD 306-37, but here extended to cover the Constantinian dynasty, AD 306-61.

Corinian: product of one of the two *officinae* based at Cirencester *(Corinium)* in the first half of the fourth century.

Cornucopia: the horn of plenty, symbol of abundance.

Cornice: linear pattern of circles enclosing petals which alternate with 'spikes'. Originally moulded decoration for ceilings.

Dionysus: Greek god of immortality around whom a frenzied cult was based. Equated with Bacchus, the Roman god of wine.

Durnovarian: product of the *officina* based at Dorchester *(Durnovaria)* in the second and third quarters of the fourth century.

Durobrivan: product of the *officina* based at Water Newton *(Durobrivae)*, Cambridgeshire, in the third quarter of the fourth century.

Durotrigan Group: largely the series of mosaics hitherto described as the 'Durnovarian School' but here comprising *officinae* based at Dorchester *(Durnovaria)* and Ilchester *(Lindinis).*

Emblema: prefabricated panel of fine mosaic set in a marble or terracotta tray, then laid into a tessellated floor. Plural: *emblemata.*

Erotes: representations of Cupid (Eros), son of Venus.
Flavian: period .of the Flavian emperors, Vespasian, Titus and Domitian, AD 69-96.
Frigidarium: cold room of a bath-house.
Greek key: see *Maeander.*
Grid: symmetrical scheme of rectangles.
Guilloche: linear pattern, originating in textiles, composed of two twisted multicoloured strands (simple guilloche/cable) or several braided strands. A guilloche mat is composed of many interbraided strands forming a rectangle.
Hadrianic: reign of Hadrian, AD 117-38.
Hellenistic: of Greek inspiration, principally from the third to first centuries BC.
Hippocampus: sea-horse, commonly represented in marine scenes.
Iconography: the study of images; in a mosaic these are invariably based on classical mythology.
Insula: block of buildings.
Isurian-Petuarian Group: largely the series of mosaics hitherto attributed to the 'school' based at Brough-on-Humber *(Petuaria)* around the middle of the fourth century. Here including mosaics discovered at Aldborough *(Isurium).*
Lindinian: product of the *officina* based at Ilchester *(Lindinis)* in the second and third quarters of the fourth century.
Lithostroton: literally, paved with stones; in ancient world used to describe mosaic and tessellated pavements.
Lozenge: a diamond shape, eight of which form a lozenge star.
Lunette: semicircular panel.
Maeander: continuous swastikas in a linear or all-over arrangement. Simple forms known as *fret* or *Greek key.*
Maenad: frenzied female devotee of Dionysus. See *Bacchant.*
Municipium: chartered town of native origin.
Muses: nine goddesses, daughters of Zeus, who inspired the arts (hence *museum).*
Musivarius: mosaicist, a craftsman in *opus musivum.*
Nereid: sea-nymph, daughter of sea-god Nereus.
Nimbus: halo usually denoting a divinity.
Officina: workshop, i.e. of a mosaicist. In its broadest sense used instead of 'school'.
Opus musivum: literally the work of the Muses, mosaic. Originally restricted to wall and vault mosaics in glass *tesserae.*
Opus signinum: crushed brick and tile mixed with mortar for use as flooring.
Opus vermiculatum: literally worm-like work. A sinuous mosaic

technique of Hellenistic origin imitating wall painting in its tonal range.

Orpheus: Thracian musician who is often quoted as subduing the birds and beasts but who as priest of Apollo became a catalytic figure in the Orphic cult whose central divinity was Dionysus.

Pattern book: postulated collection of designs, patterns and motifs outlined on cartoons and used by mosaicists.

Pelta: semicircular shield of the Amazons stylised as a common motif in Roman art.

Prefabrication: the manufacture of mosaic panels in the workshop — known on the continent as *à rivoltatura*.

Quadrant: convex corner panel in a compass-drawn scheme.

Quarter rounding: the curved fillet of plaster sealing the junction of wall plaster and tessellation.

Roundel: circular panel of mosaic.

Saltire: design also known as a St Andrew's cross. A Corinian speciality.

Samian: red gloss tableware from Gaul, often cut into *tesserae,* from which vessel type may be identified and dated.

Satyr: male devotee of Dionysus with goat's horns and legs.

Scroll: linear pattern of vegetable character, usually a sinuous loop of whole flowers, leaves or petals (see *Acanthus*).

Spandrel: space between a circle and its containing square.

Substratum: foundation, i.e. of mosaic pavement.

Temenos: religious precinct.

Tessera, tessella: literally, a tablet of stone. Generally a tailored stone for a mosaic or tessellated pavement.

Thiasos: a triumph, i.e. a lively procession, involving Dionysus or, if a marine *thiasos,* Neptune and Amphitrite.

Triclinium: dining room, strictly for three couches.

10
Bibliography

Antiquarian

Fowler, W. *Twenty-six Plates of Mosaic Pavements.* 1796–1818.
Lysons, S. *Roman Antiquities at Woodchester.* 1797.
Lysons, S. *Reliquae Britannico-Romanae*, Volumes 1–3. 1813-17.
Morgan, T. *Romano-British Mosaic Pavements.* Whiting and Co., 1886.

General

Dunbabin, K.M.D. Mosaics of the Greek & Roman World. Cambridge, 1999.
Neal, D. *Roman Mosaics in Britain.* Britannia Monograph Series Number 1, 1981.

Rainey, A. *Mosaics in Roman Britain: A Gazetteer*. David and Charles, 1973.

Smith, D.J. 'Mosaics' in Henig, M. (editor) *A Handbook of Roman Art*. Phaidon, 1983, 116-38.

Toynbee, J.M.C. 'Floor Mosaics' in *Art in Britain under the Romans*. Clarendon, 1964.

Witts, P. *Mosaics in Roman Britain: Stories in Stone*. Stroud, 2005.

Schools and Officinae

Branigan, K. 'Mosaics in Roman Britain: Schools, Symbols and Service'. *Mosaic* 18, 1991, 9–14.

Cosh, S. 'The Lindinis brand of the Corinian Saltire Officina' in *Mosaic* 16, 1989, 6–9.

Cosh, S. 'A new look at the Corinian Saltire school'. *Mosaic* 19, 1992, 7–10.

Johnson, P. 'The Ilchester-Lindinis Officina'. *Mosaic* 8, April 1983, 5–8.

Johnson, P. 'Town mosaics and urban officina' in Greep, S. (editor) *Roman Towns: The Wheeler Inheritance*. 1993, 147–65.

Smith, D.J. 'Roman Mosaics in Britain before the Fourth Century' in Stern, H. (editor) *La Mosaique Greco-Romaine, Volume 2*, Editions Picard, Paris, 269–90.

Studies in Iconography

Beeson, A.J. 'A Terracotta Goddess from Agrigento and the Venus from Hemsworth'. *Mosaic* 28, 2001, 20–21.

Eriksen, R.T. 'Syncretistic Symbolism and the Christian Roman Mosaic at Hinton St Mary: A Closer Reading'. *Proceedings Dorset Natural History and Archaeological Society*, Volume 102, 1980, 43–8.

Henig, M. 'Romano-British Mosaics and Romano-Celtic Religion'. *ARA: The Bulletin of the Association for Roman Archaeology* 11, Aug 2001, 12–14.

Ling, R. 'The Bellerophon Mosaic at Frampton: Inscriptions and Programmatic Content'. *Mosaic* 34, 2007, 5–11.

Ling, R. 'The Seasons in Romano-British Mosaic Pavements.' *Britannia*, Volume XIV, 1983, 13–21.

Neal, D.S. and Cosh, S. 'Daphne at Dinnington'. *Mosaic* 32, 2005, 23–25.

Stupperich, R. 'Some Fourth–Century British Mosaics Reconsidered.' *Britannia, Volume XI*, 1980, 289–301.

Witts, P. 'Nymphs and Shepherds? A re-evaluation of scenes in mosaics from Brading, Frampton and Pitney'. *Mosaic* 33, 2006, 17–20.

Walters, B. 'The Orpheus Mosaic in Littlecote Park, England' in Campanati, R. (editor) *Atti del III Colloquio Internazionale sul Mosaico Antico*, Mario Lapucci, Edizioni del Girasole, Bologna, 1984, 433–42.

Chronology

Johnson, P. 'Legionary Mosaics in Chester'. *Mosaic* 10, April 1984, 6–8.

Johnson, P. 'The Mosaics of Bignor Villa, England: A Gallo-Roman Connection' in Campanati, R. *op.cit.*, 405–10.

Johnson, P, 'Some Chronological Problems in the Study of Romano-British Mosaics' in

proceedings of *IV Internationales Mosaikkolloquium*, Trier, 1984.
Neal, D.S. 'The Roman Mosaics from Verulamium'. *ASPROM Mosaics Journal* 25, 1998, 15–23.
Smith, D.J. 'Roman Mosaics in Britain before the Fourth Century' in Stern, H. 1975, *op.cit*,
Smith, D.J. ' Romano-British Mosaics in the Third Century; in King, A. and Henig, M. (editors) *The Roman West in the Third Century*. British Archaeological Reports, International Series, No. 109, 1981, 159–65.

General Research

Cookson, N. 'Romano-British Mosaics: A Reassessment and Critique of some Notable Stylistic Affinities.' *British Archaeological Report*, 135, 1984.
Henig, M. 'Religion and Mosaics in Roman Britain'. *Mosaic* 16, 1989, 6–9.
Ling, R. 'Mosaics in Roman Britain: Discussions and Research since 1945'. *Britannia* 28, 1997, 259–295.
Scott, S. *Art and Society in Fourth-Century Britain: Villa Mosaics in Context.* Oxford University School of Archaeology Monograph no. 53, Oxford, 2000.
Tebby, S. *Geometric Design in Roman Tesselated Pavements.* (updated edition) Lutterworth, 2003.
Witts, P. 'Mosaics and Room Function: the evidence from some fourth-century Romano-British mosaics'. *Britannia* 31, 2000, 291–324.

Technical

Journal of Mosaic Research, Vol. 1-2, Uludag University Mosaic Research Centre, Turkey, 2008.
Michaelides, D. (editor) *Mosaics Make A Site: The Conservation in Situ of Mosaics on Archaeological Sites. Proceedings of the VI ICCM Conference 1996.* Rome, 2003.
Mosaics Number 1: Deterioriation and Conservation. ICCROM, Rome. Papers of the First International Symposium on the Conservation of Mosaics, Rome, 1977.
Mosaics Number 2: Safeguard. ICCROM, Rome. Volume of guidelines by the International Committee for the Conservation of Mosaics, 1978 and 1980.
Mosaics Number 3: Conservation in Situ. ICCROM, Rome. Papers of the Second General Conference of the International Committee for the Conservation of Mosaics at Aquileia, 1983.
Neal, D.S and Cosh, S. *Corpus of Romano-British Mosaics*, in 4 volumes, published by the Society of Antiquaries of London, under the auspices of ASPROM:
Vol. 1 : Northern Britain including the Midlands and East Anglia, London, 2002.
Vol. 2: South-West Britain, London, 2005.
Vol. 3: South-East Britain, London, 2009.
Vol. 4: Western Britain, including Wales, London, 2010.

Contacts

ASPROM, the Association for the Study and Preservation of Roman Mosaics, publishes an annual illustrated bulletin, Mosaic, and organises regular meetings and symposia. Details from Honorary Secretary Dr Janet Huskinson, 61 Norwich Street, Cambridge CB2 1ND.

Index